Unveiling the Shadows: A Journey into Financial Crimes and Scandals

Edward Turner

Published by Oliver Lancaster, 2023.

While every precaution has been taken in the preparation of this book, the publisher assumes no responsibility for errors or omissions, or for damages resulting from the use of the information contained herein.

UNVEILING THE SHADOWS: A JOURNEY INTO FINANCIAL CRIMES AND SCANDALS

First edition. July 8, 2023.

Copyright © 2023 Edward Turner.

ISBN: 979-8223284642

Written by Edward Turner.

Also by Edward Turner

Ghosts of Paris: Ten Haunted Places in the City of Love
Appalachian Nightmares: The Top 10 Creepy Creatures of the
Mountains
Asia's Top Ten Cryptids: Legends, Sightings, and Theories
Beyond the Shadows: Unlocking the Mystery of Bigfoot
Evil Women in History: Uncovering the Gruesome Crimes of
Ten Notorious Female Killers
Ghosts of London: Ten Haunted Places in The City
Ghosts of New York: Ten Haunted Places in The Big Apple
Ghosts of Oregon: The Top 10 Haunted Places You Must
Visit
Ghosts of the Stage: Ten Hauntings at the Theatre
Missouri Nightmares: The Top 10 Chilling Legends
Mothman Unleashed: Into the Darkened Skies
North America's Top Ten Cryptids: Legends, Sightings, and
Theories
Philly's Phantom Encounters: Exploring the City's Most
Haunted Places
Secrets of the Deep: The Mystery of the Loch Ness Monster
Unsolved Mysteries: Delving into the Shadows of Infamous
Murders and Enigmatic Killers
Unveiling the Shadows: A Journey into Financial Crimes and
Scandals

Unveiling the Shadows: A Journey into Financial Crimes and Scandals

Disclaimer: The following book is intended for informational purposes only. The content provided is based on extensive research and general knowledge. The aim of this book is to shed light on notable cases of financial fraud, embezzlement, insider trading, money laundering, tax evasion, and elite sex trafficking and exploitation. It is important to note that the individuals mentioned in this book, such as Bernard Madoff, Martha Stewart, Lionel Messi, and Jeffrey Epstein, have been widely reported in the media and their actions have been subject to legal proceedings, public scrutiny, and various accounts. However, the author of this book does not assume responsibility for the accuracy, completeness, or current status of the information provided regarding these individuals. The events, actions, and circumstances surrounding these individuals have been extensively covered by news outlets, investigative reports, and legal documents. The information presented in this book is based on public records and available sources, and any opinions expressed are solely those of the author and do not constitute legal or professional advice.Furthermore, the author does not endorse or support the actions, behaviours, or beliefs of the individuals discussed in this book. The purpose of including their stories is to provide an overview of notable cases that have had significant impacts on society, the financial industry, and the justice system.It is crucial to seek professional advice or consult trusted sources for any legal, financial, or personal matters discussed in this book. The author encourages readers to conduct their own research and due diligence to obtain up-to-date and accurate information.The author and publisher disclaim any liability or responsibility for any errors, omissions, or inaccuracies in the information provided within this book. The reader assumes all risks and responsibilities for their own actions and decisions based on the information presented herein.Lastly, this book does not aim to pass judgement or make definitive conclusions about the guilt or innocence of the individuals mentioned. Legal determinations and court verdicts are the proper authorities to establish guilt or innocence in accordance with the law.By reading this book, you acknowledge and agree to the terms of this disclaimer.

UNVEILING THE SHADOWS: A JOURNEY INTO FINANCIAL CRIMES AND SCANDALS

UNVEILING THE SHADOWS: A JOURNEY INTO FINANCIAL CRIMES AND SCANDALS

Introduction

In a world driven by wealth, power, and secrecy, the dark underbelly of financial crimes and scandals often remains hidden from the public eye. Behind the scenes, influential individuals orchestrate intricate schemes, exploiting loopholes and engaging in illicit activities that shake the foundations of our financial systems. Unveiling the Shadows takes you on a captivating journey into the depths of some of the most notorious cases, exposing the shocking realities and profound consequences of these acts.

Financial crimes and scandals have plagued societies for centuries, leaving a trail of shattered lives and shattered trust in their wake. From fraudulent Ponzi schemes to insider trading, money laundering, tax evasion, and even the disturbing world of elite sex trafficking, these chapters will delve into the intricate web of deceit and manipulation that has ensnared both the powerful and the vulnerable.

The aim of this book is to shed light on the intricate mechanisms and underlying motivations that drive these crimes. Through meticulously researched accounts, we will explore the individuals behind the scandals, the strategies they employed, and the far-reaching impact their actions had on both individuals and society at large. By understanding these cases, we hope to raise awareness, encourage discussion, and prompt reflection on the broader issues surrounding financial crimes and the urgent need for reform.

Each chapter focuses on a distinct area of financial crime, exploring a specific case that exemplifies the depth of the problem. From the audacious Ponzi scheme orchestrated by Bernard Madoff, to Martha Stewart's insider trading scandal, the Panama Papers' exposure of money laundering networks, Lionel Messi's brush with tax evasion, and the horrifying world of sex trafficking and exploitation associated with Jeffrey Epstein, these stories will captivate readers while shedding light on the complex issues at hand.

As we embark on this journey, we must acknowledge that these cases represent just a fraction of the financial crimes and scandals that persist worldwide. By uncovering the truth and examining the consequences, we hope to inspire change, fuel public discourse, and foster a greater sense of accountability within our financial systems. Unveiling the Shadows invites you to explore the dark side of finance, challenging the status quo and sparking a collective call for justice and reform.

Chapter 1: Financial Fraud and Embezzlement - Bernard "Bernie" Madoff

Bernard Lawrence Madoff, commonly known as Bernie Madoff, is a name that has become synonymous with one of the most audacious and far-reaching financial frauds in history. Born on April 29, 1938, in Queens, New York, Madoff rose to prominence as a respected financier and former chairman of the NASDAQ stock exchange. However, beneath the veneer of success and influence, a complex web of deception and deceit was being spun, leading to the devastating unravelling of his fraudulent empire.

In the annals of financial fraud, Madoff's Ponzi scheme stands as a stark reminder of the profound damage that can be inflicted upon unsuspecting investors. Spanning over several decades, Madoff's scheme defrauded thousands of individuals, charities, and even celebrities of billions of dollars. The scope and audacity of his scheme, which lasted from the early 1990s until his arrest in December 2008, sent shockwaves throughout the financial world and left an indelible mark on the collective consciousness.

To truly understand the impact and magnitude of Madoff's fraud, it is essential to delve into the intricacies of his scheme and examine the factors that allowed it to persist undetected for so long. At its core, a Ponzi scheme is a fraudulent investment operation in which returns for older investors are paid using funds contributed by new investors, rather than from legitimate profits. Madoff's scheme was no different, with new investor funds being used to pay off previous investors, creating the illusion of consistent and lucrative returns.

Madoff employed a mix of charm, expertise, and trust to lure in a diverse range of investors, from Wall Street executives to ordinary individuals seeking secure and reliable investment opportunities. His reputation as a highly successful and reputable figure within the financial industry, coupled with consistent returns even in times of economic downturn, engendered a sense of confidence and trust among his clients. Little did they know that their investments were being syphoned off to sustain the illusion of a profitable enterprise.

The operation of Madoff's Ponzi scheme was shrouded in secrecy and carefully constructed deception. Fake account statements were generated, showcasing consistent and impressive returns that mesmerised investors and further solidified their trust. Madoff even enlisted the aid of his family members, including his brother Peter Madoff, to manage various aspects of the scheme and perpetuate the façade of legitimacy.

As the scheme grew in complexity and size, so did the number of victims ensnared in its web. Charitable organisations, such as the Elie Wiesel Foundation and the Picower Foundation, suffered substantial losses, impacting their ability to support causes they held dear. Celebrities, including actors Kevin Bacon and Kyra Sedgwick, also found themselves among the victims of Madoff's deceit. The extent of the devastation caused by Madoff's fraud reached far and wide, leaving lives in ruins and countless dreams shattered.

The unravelling of Madoff's scheme occurred amidst the backdrop of the global financial crisis in 2008. As economic uncertainties heightened, some investors sought to withdraw their investments, triggering a chain of events that would expose Madoff's fraudulent activities. On December 11, 2008, Madoff was arrested and charged with securities fraud, investment advisor fraud, and other related offences. The staggering extent of the losses suffered by his investors soon became apparent, with estimates suggesting that the total amount defrauded could exceed $65 billion.

The impact of Madoff's fraud reverberated far beyond the financial losses. It eroded public trust in the financial industry, undermined regulatory bodies, and prompted soul-searching within both the investment community and the broader public. Questions were raised about the effectiveness of oversight mechanisms and the need for stronger regulations to prevent similar catastrophes in the future.

Bernie Madoff's name will forever be etched in history as a cautionary tale of greed, betrayal, and the devastating consequences of unchecked financial deception. As we explore the intricate details of his Ponzi scheme and examine the aftermath of his arrest and conviction, we must confront the fundamental questions about the nature of trust, the role of regulation, and the pursuit of justice within our financial systems. The tale of Bernie Madoff serves as a reminder that vigilance, transparency, and ethical conduct are essential to safeguarding the integrity of our financial institutions and protecting the interests of investors worldwide.

The rise and fall of Bernard Madoff's financial empire

BERNARD "BERNIE" MADOFF'S rise to prominence in the financial world was as remarkable as it was deceitful. Over several decades, he carefully constructed an intricate web of deception, luring in investors and amassing a financial empire built on fraud and false promises. The audacity and duration of Madoff's scheme have left many wondering how he managed to deceive investors for so long.

Madoff's journey into financial fraud began in the early 1960s when he founded Bernard L. Madoff Investment Securities LLC. Initially, the firm operated as a legitimate market-making and trading business, gaining recognition and respect within the industry. Madoff himself was well-regarded and served as the chairman of the NASDAQ stock exchange from 1990 to 1993, further enhancing his reputation and visibility.

One of the key factors that enabled Madoff to deceive investors for an extended period was the trust he carefully cultivated. He positioned himself as a trustworthy and experienced financier, playing on his established reputation and involvement in the financial community. Madoff targeted a diverse range of investors, including wealthy individuals, charitable organisations, and even celebrities, exploiting their trust in him as a reputable figure.

Another critical aspect of Madoff's scheme was the consistency of his returns. Investors were lured in by the promise of steady and impressive profits, even in times of economic uncertainty. Madoff claimed to employ a sophisticated investment strategy, using a split-strike conversion technique and generating consistent returns regardless of market conditions. This illusion of reliability and consistency enticed investors, making them more willing to overlook red flags or conduct thorough due diligence.

To perpetuate the illusion of success, Madoff produced fraudulent account statements. These statements showcased consistent and often extraordinary returns, bolstering investor confidence and creating a sense of security. Many investors, relying solely on these statements as evidence of their investments' performance, did not question or scrutinise Madoff's activities further. The production of these falsified documents required a careful orchestration of deceit, involving the collaboration of employees and the manipulation of records.

Furthermore, Madoff instilled a sense of exclusivity and secrecy around his investment strategy. He limited access to his fund, creating an air of mystique and making it seem like a privilege to invest with him. This exclusivity created a perception that the investments were in high demand, fostering an environment where investors felt fortunate to be a part of Madoff's exclusive circle.

Madoff also used a classic element of a Ponzi scheme—paying off early investors with funds from new investors. By providing consistent returns to those who chose to withdraw their investments, he perpetuated the illusion of a successful enterprise. These satisfied early investors acted as unintentional accomplices, unknowingly vouching for the legitimacy of Madoff's operation when interacting with potential new investors.

Moreover, Madoff skillfully exploited the absence of effective regulatory oversight. Despite the SEC receiving warnings and red flags regarding his activities, their investigations failed to uncover the truth. Madoff adeptly manipulated and deceived regulators, evading detection and continuing his fraudulent activities.

The scheme eventually began to unravel in the wake of the global financial crisis in 2008. As economic uncertainties mounted, some investors sought to withdraw their investments from Madoff's fund. However, the financial crisis made it increasingly difficult for Madoff to secure new investments to sustain the scheme. This led to a cascade of withdrawals and the eventual exposure of his fraudulent activities.

In December 2008, Madoff was arrested and charged with securities fraud, investment advisor fraud, and other related offences. The scope of the fraud was staggering, with estimates suggesting that the total losses suffered by investors could exceed $65 billion.

Bernard Madoff's ability to deceive investors for such an extended period was a result of various factors working in conjunction. These included his established reputation, the illusion of consistency and reliability, the production of fraudulent account statements, the exclusivity and secrecy surrounding his operations, the use of early investors to attract new investors, and the absence of effective regulatory oversight. Madoff's scheme ultimately collapsed in the face of economic challenges, exposing the depth of his deception and leaving behind a legacy of shattered lives and shattered trust. The Madoff case serves as a stark reminder of the need for vigilance, transparency, and robust regulatory measures to safeguard investors and maintain the integrity of our financial systems.

The consequences of Madoff's Ponzi scheme

THE CONSEQUENCES OF Bernard Madoff's Ponzi scheme reverberated far beyond the financial losses suffered by his victims. The impact extended to the victims themselves, the financial industry, and the regulatory landscape, leaving a lasting imprint on all aspects of the financial world.

First and foremost, the victims of Madoff's scheme bore the brunt of the devastating consequences. Thousands of individuals and entities, including retirees, charities, and institutional investors, found their savings and investments wiped out. The financial losses were staggering, with estimates suggesting that the total amount defrauded could exceed $65 billion. Many victims faced severe financial hardship, having entrusted their life savings and future security to Madoff's false promises.

The psychological and emotional toll on the victims cannot be understated. The realisation that their trust had been betrayed, coupled with the sense of powerlessness and vulnerability, caused immeasurable distress. Some victims faced financial ruin, losing their homes, businesses, and livelihoods. Others struggled with feelings of shame, guilt, and betrayal, as they grappled with the aftermath of the scheme. The impact on their lives was profound and long-lasting.

The Madoff Ponzi scheme had significant repercussions for the financial industry as a whole. It eroded public trust and confidence in the integrity of financial institutions and investment advisors. Investors became more sceptical and cautious, demanding greater transparency and due diligence in their investment decisions. The reputational damage inflicted by Madoff's fraud extended beyond his own firm, casting a shadow of suspicion over the entire financial industry.

The case exposed critical weaknesses in the regulatory landscape and led to a reevaluation of oversight mechanisms. The Securities and Exchange Commission (SEC), in particular, faced substantial criticism for its failure to detect and prevent Madoff's scheme despite receiving multiple warnings and red flags. The regulatory landscape was seen as inadequate, with deficiencies in the SEC's enforcement capabilities and oversight processes. The Madoff case became a catalyst for regulatory reforms, prompting calls for increased transparency, stronger investor protections, and more stringent regulatory measures.

In response to the Madoff scandal, regulatory bodies implemented several reforms to enhance investor safeguards. The Dodd-Frank Wall Street Reform and Consumer Protection Act, enacted in 2010, introduced comprehensive financial regulations aimed at preventing fraud, improving transparency, and strengthening oversight. The act established the Financial Stability Oversight Council (FSOC) to monitor and address systemic risks within the financial industry. It also created the Consumer Financial Protection Bureau (CFPB) to protect consumers from abusive financial practices.

The Madoff case also highlighted the need for greater coordination and information sharing among regulatory bodies. The Financial Industry Regulatory Authority (FINRA) and other self-regulatory organisations bolstered their efforts to detect and deter fraud within the financial industry. The SEC implemented measures to improve its examination and enforcement capabilities, seeking to prevent future Ponzi schemes and fraudulent activities.

Furthermore, the Madoff case served as a wake-up call for investors to exercise greater caution and conduct thorough due diligence. It emphasised the importance of diversification, scepticism towards unusually high or consistent returns, and the necessity of verifying the legitimacy of investment opportunities. Investors became more vigilant, demanding increased transparency and accountability from financial institutions and advisors.

Overall, the consequences of Madoff's Ponzi scheme were far-reaching and profound. The victims suffered devastating financial losses and endured significant emotional turmoil. The financial industry faced reputational damage and scrutiny, leading to increased demands for transparency and accountability. The regulatory landscape underwent reforms aimed at strengthening oversight and investor protections. The Madoff case served as a catalyst for change, prompting a collective reassessment of the financial industry's practices and the need for robust regulatory measures to safeguard against future fraud and deception.

What allowed Madoff's fraud to go undetected?

THE FACTORS THAT ALLOWED Bernard Madoff's Ponzi scheme to go undetected for an extended period were a combination of deliberate deception, regulatory shortcomings, and missed warning signs. While the full extent of Madoff's fraudulent activities was ultimately exposed, there were several factors that contributed to the scheme remaining undetected for so long.

One of the key factors was Madoff's ability to exploit the trust and reputation he had built over the years. As a former chairman of the NASDAQ stock exchange and a respected figure in the financial industry, Madoff was able to leverage his established reputation to lure in investors. Many investors were drawn to him based on the perception that he was a reputable and experienced financier. This trust and credibility shielded him from initial suspicion and allowed the scheme to persist.

Another factor that contributed to the fraud going undetected was Madoff's deliberate efforts to maintain an air of exclusivity and secrecy around his investment strategy. He limited access to his fund, creating a sense of privilege and scarcity among potential investors. This exclusivity made the investments seem highly sought-after and valuable, further cementing the perception of legitimacy. By carefully selecting his clients and screening out those who may have been more likely to scrutinise his operations, Madoff minimised the risk of exposure.

Additionally, Madoff took advantage of the complexity and opacity of his investment strategy to discourage scrutiny. He claimed to employ a sophisticated split-strike conversion technique, which he said allowed for consistent returns regardless of market conditions. This complexity made it difficult for investors and even regulatory bodies to fully understand the inner workings of his operations. Madoff capitalised on this confusion, using technical jargon and complex explanations to deter further inquiries.

Another crucial factor was the production of fraudulent account statements. Madoff and his team generated false documents that showcased consistent and impressive returns for investors. These statements provided a false sense of security, making it appear as though the investments were performing well. Many investors relied solely on these statements without conducting further due diligence, which allowed the scheme to continue unchallenged.

Regulatory shortcomings and missed warning signs also played a significant role in Madoff's fraud going undetected. Despite receiving multiple warnings and red flags, the Securities and Exchange Commission (SEC) failed to uncover the truth behind Madoff's operations. Over the years, the SEC conducted several investigations into Madoff's activities, but each time they failed to detect the fraud. The regulatory oversight was hindered by a lack of resources, expertise, and coordination, allowing Madoff to evade detection.

Several whistleblowers and analysts raised concerns and suspicions about Madoff's operations over the years, but their warnings were largely dismissed or ignored. Harry Markopolos, a financial analyst, repeatedly tried to alert the SEC to the fraudulent nature of Madoff's scheme. Markopolos submitted detailed reports outlining his findings, but the SEC did not take immediate action. The failure to heed these warnings was a significant missed opportunity to expose the fraud earlier.

In hindsight, there were warning signs that, if recognized earlier, could have potentially exposed Madoff's scheme. The consistent and unusually high returns, the lack of transparency regarding the investment strategy, the absence of independent custodians for investor funds, and the consistent resistance to external audits were all red flags that should have raised suspicions. However, these warning signs were either overlooked or not thoroughly investigated, allowing the fraud to continue.

The factors that allowed Madoff's fraud to go undetected for so long were a combination of his ability to exploit trust and reputation, the exclusivity and secrecy surrounding his operations, the complexity of his investment strategy, the production of fraudulent account statements, regulatory shortcomings, and missed warning signs. The case of Bernard Madoff serves as a stark reminder of the importance of robust regulation, investor scepticism, and the need for thorough due diligence to protect against fraudulent schemes in the financial industry.

What followed?

IN THE WAKE OF BERNARD Madoff's financial fraud and embezzlement, there are valuable lessons to be learned. This chapter has shed light on the intricate details of Madoff's Ponzi scheme and the devastating consequences it had on investors, the financial industry, and regulatory oversight. As we reflect on the implications of this crime, several key learnings emerge, highlighting the need for increased vigilance, transparency, and accountability within our financial systems.

One crucial lesson is the importance of investor due diligence. Madoff's scheme flourished because investors placed unwavering trust in his reputation and failed to conduct thorough investigations into his operations. The allure of consistent and impressive returns blinded many to the warning signs and prevented them from asking critical questions. It is essential for investors to recognize that even the most reputable individuals or institutions can engage in fraudulent activities. Conducting thorough research, verifying information independently, and seeking multiple sources of advice can help mitigate the risk of falling victim to such schemes.

Transparency and accountability are paramount in maintaining the integrity of our financial institutions. Madoff's ability to deceive investors for so long was, in part, facilitated by the lack of transparency surrounding his operations. The complexity of his investment strategy, the production of fraudulent account statements, and the absence of independent audits all contributed to the scheme's longevity. To prevent similar crimes in the future, financial institutions must be transparent about their operations and provide investors with accessible and accurate information. External audits and regulatory oversight are essential to ensure that financial institutions adhere to ethical standards and are held accountable for their actions.

The case of Bernard Madoff also exposed critical weaknesses in regulatory oversight. The Securities and Exchange Commission (SEC) failed to detect and prevent the fraud, despite receiving numerous warnings and red flags. This highlights the need for stronger regulatory measures and enhanced coordination among regulatory bodies. Regulators should have the necessary resources, expertise, and authority to effectively investigate and uncover fraudulent activities. Improved collaboration and information sharing between regulatory agencies can aid in identifying patterns and detecting fraudulent schemes earlier.

Furthermore, the Madoff case emphasises the importance of fostering a culture of whistleblowing. Whistleblowers, such as

Harry Markopolos, played a vital role in bringing Madoff's fraud to light. Their courage in speaking out against wrongdoing should be encouraged and protected. Robust whistleblower protection laws and mechanisms can incentivize individuals to come forward with valuable information, acting as a critical check on fraudulent activities.

Education and awareness are fundamental in preventing financial fraud. Investors, particularly those who may be more vulnerable to scams, should be equipped with the knowledge and tools to make informed decisions. Promoting financial literacy programs and resources can empower individuals to recognize warning signs, understand investment risks, and protect themselves from fraudulent schemes.

The consequences of Madoff's scheme extended beyond financial losses. The emotional and psychological toll on the victims was significant, highlighting the need for empathy and support for those affected by financial crimes. Offering resources for victims, such as counselling services and financial assistance, can aid in their recovery and rebuilding process.

Ultimately, the Madoff case serves as a wake-up call to individuals, financial institutions, and regulators. It underscores the importance of maintaining trust, integrity, and accountability within our financial systems. By learning from the lessons exposed by this crime, we can work towards creating a more transparent, resilient, and ethical financial environment.

As we conclude this chapter on financial fraud and embezzlement, it is crucial to recognize that the Madoff case is not an isolated incident. It represents a broader challenge faced by society in combating financial crimes. By implementing the learnings from this case, we can take significant strides towards preventing future frauds, protecting investors, and preserving the integrity of our financial systems.

Chapter 2: Insider Trading - Martha Stewart

Martha Stewart, a prominent figure in the world of business and media, is widely recognized as one of the most successful entrepreneurs and lifestyle gurus of her time. Born on August 3, 1941, in Jersey City, New Jersey, Martha Helen Kostyra Stewart built an empire centred around homemaking, cooking, entertaining, and crafts.

From a young age, Stewart demonstrated a keen eye for aesthetics and a passion for creating beautiful and functional spaces. She initially pursued a career in modelling, working for well-known clients such as Chanel and Calvin Klein. However, it was her venture into the world of homemaking and creative arts that truly propelled her to fame and fortune.

Stewart's entrepreneurial journey began in the late 1970s when she started a catering business, which soon evolved into a successful line of gourmet food products. Her attention to detail, impeccable taste, and ability to curate stylish experiences garnered attention and attracted a dedicated following.

In 1982, Stewart published her first book, "Entertaining," which quickly became a bestseller. This marked the beginning of her foray into publishing, as she continued to release a series of successful books on topics ranging from cooking and entertaining to home décor and gardening. Stewart's books became go-to resources for individuals seeking guidance on creating a beautiful and organised home.

Recognizing the power of television as a medium, Stewart made her way into the world of broadcasting. In 1993, she launched "Martha Stewart Living," a television show that showcased her expertise in various aspects of domestic life. The show, which focused on cooking, crafts, and home improvement, quickly gained a loyal viewership and earned numerous accolades, including several Daytime Emmy Awards.

Alongside her television show, Stewart expanded her media presence through the launch of "Martha Stewart Living" magazine in 1990. The magazine became an essential resource for individuals seeking inspiration for their homes and everyday lives. Stewart's brand continued to grow with the establishment of the Martha Stewart Living Omnimedia company, which encompassed television, publishing, merchandising, and digital media.

Stewart's influence extended beyond the realms of homemaking and media. She leveraged her brand to partner with various companies, endorsing and creating product lines ranging from home goods and kitchen appliances to bedding and furniture. Stewart's name became synonymous with quality, elegance, and an aspirational lifestyle.

However, alongside her remarkable success, Martha Stewart faced a significant setback in her career that would forever alter her public image. In 2001, she became embroiled in an insider trading scandal involving the sale of shares in ImClone

Systems, a biopharmaceutical company. Stewart's actions surrounding the sale of these shares led to charges of securities fraud, obstruction of justice, and making false statements.

The legal battle and subsequent conviction cast a shadow over Stewart's reputation and career. In 2004, she was found guilty on all counts and sentenced to five months in prison, a period of supervised release, and financial penalties. Despite the challenges she faced, Stewart displayed resilience and determination, working to rebuild her brand and regain public trust after serving her sentence.

Today, Martha Stewart remains a respected figure in the business and media world. She continues to share her expertise through various platforms, including her website, social media, and television appearances. Stewart's influence and legacy extend beyond her personal achievements, as she has inspired countless individuals to embrace creativity, cultivate beautiful living spaces, and pursue their passions.

Martha Stewart's journey from a model to a household name and business magnate is a testament to her entrepreneurial spirit, creativity, and perseverance. Despite facing a significant setback in her career, Stewart's impact on the world of homemaking, cooking, and lifestyle remains enduring. Through her books, television shows, and media empire, she has inspired millions of individuals to find joy in creating beautiful, well-curated homes and lives.

How did Martha Stewart become involved in insider trading?

THE MARTHA STEWART insider trading case captivated the public's attention and sent shockwaves through the business and media world. Martha Stewart, a renowned American businesswoman and media personality, became embroiled in a scandal that ultimately led to her conviction on charges related to insider trading.

Stewart's involvement in insider trading began with her connection to ImClone Systems, a biopharmaceutical company led by her friend, Samuel Waksal. In December 2001, ImClone's experimental cancer drug, Erbitux, faced a setback when the U.S. Food and Drug Administration (FDA) announced it would not review the drug's application for approval. Waksal, having prior knowledge of the FDA's decision, attempted to sell his shares of ImClone before the public announcement, leading to suspicions of insider trading.

It was during this period that Stewart received a phone call from her broker, Peter Bacanovic, at Merrill Lynch. Bacanovic informed Stewart that Waksal was attempting to sell his shares, prompting Stewart to sell her own 3,928 ImClone shares. Stewart's decision to sell raised suspicions, as it suggested that she may have received non-public information about the FDA's decision.

The specific charges against Stewart stemmed from her actions surrounding the sale of her ImClone shares. Stewart was charged with securities fraud, obstruction of justice, and making false statements to federal investigators. The charges revolved around her alleged attempts to cover up her actions and mislead investigators during the subsequent investigation.

Stewart was accused of engaging in a conspiracy to deceive investigators by providing false and misleading statements about her reasons for selling the ImClone shares. She claimed that the decision to sell was based on a pre-existing agreement with Bacanovic to sell the shares if they fell below $60. However, evidence presented during the trial suggested that this agreement did not exist and that Stewart sold the shares based on the inside information she received.

During the trial, the government presented phone records, witness testimonies, and other evidence to build their case against Stewart. The prosecution argued that Stewart had a clear motive to sell her shares based on insider information and that she took deliberate steps to conceal her true reasons for selling.

The case against Stewart was closely followed by the media, given her prominent status as a successful businesswoman and television personality. The trial and subsequent conviction of Stewart drew significant attention and generated debates about the ethics of insider trading and the appropriate punishment for such offences.

In March 2004, Martha Stewart was found guilty on all counts and sentenced to five months in prison, two years of supervised release, and a financial penalty. She served her sentence at a federal prison camp in Alderson, West Virginia, and was released in March 2005.

The Martha Stewart insider trading case had a profound impact on Stewart's personal and professional life. She faced significant reputational damage, and her media empire suffered as a result of the scandal. However, Stewart managed to rebuild her brand and regain some public support after her release from prison, continuing her successful career in the media and business industries.

The case also had broader implications, serving as a high-profile example of the consequences of engaging in insider trading. It highlighted the importance of maintaining integrity in financial markets and the legal ramifications faced by individuals who trade based on non-public information.

The Martha Stewart insider trading case arose from her involvement with ImClone Systems and the sale of her shares based on non-public information. The specific charges against Stewart included securities fraud, obstruction of justice, and making false statements. The case attracted significant attention and sparked discussions about the ethics of insider trading and the accountability of high-profile individuals. Stewart's conviction and subsequent prison sentence had lasting consequences for her personal and professional life, serving as a reminder of the legal and reputational risks associated with insider trading.

The legal and ethical implications of insider trading

INSIDER TRADING IS a practice that involves the buying or selling of securities based on material, non-public information about a company. It is widely considered a serious offence due to its detrimental effects on the integrity and fairness of financial markets. The legal and ethical implications of insider trading are significant, as they undermine investor confidence, distort market efficiency, and create unfair advantages for those who possess privileged information.

One of the primary reasons insider trading is considered a serious offence is because it violates the principles of fairness and equal opportunity. Financial markets are built on the foundation of transparency and equal access to information. Insider trading disrupts this balance by allowing individuals with non-public information to gain an unfair advantage over other market participants. This selective disclosure of information erodes trust and confidence in the market, as it creates a perception that the playing field is not level.

Moreover, insider trading can lead to market manipulation and distort the efficient allocation of resources. When individuals trade based on insider information, they can drive up or down the price of securities, misrepresenting their true value. This manipulation can harm investors who are not privy to the insider information, as they make investment decisions based on inaccurate or incomplete information. The resulting distortion in prices undermines the efficient functioning of markets and hinders the allocation of capital to its most productive uses.

From a legal standpoint, insider trading is prohibited in most jurisdictions due to its potential for unfair enrichment and the erosion of investor trust. Laws and regulations surrounding insider trading vary across countries, but they generally aim to prevent individuals from trading on non-public material information and require the disclosure of such information to the public in a fair and timely manner. Violations of insider trading laws can lead to severe penalties, including financial fines, imprisonment, and reputational damage.

The ethical implications of insider trading stem from the principles of integrity, honesty, and fiduciary duty. Corporate insiders, such as executives, directors, and employees, owe a duty of loyalty and fiduciary responsibility to their companies and shareholders. Engaging in insider trading violates this duty by exploiting privileged information for personal gain at the expense of others. It represents a breach of trust and undermines the ethical obligations individuals have to act in the best interests of shareholders and maintain the integrity of the capital markets.

Insider trading also has broader implications for market efficiency and investor confidence. When investors perceive that insider trading is prevalent and goes unpunished, it erodes trust in the fairness and integrity of the market. Investors may become reluctant to participate in the market, fearing that they are at a disadvantage and that their investments may be subject to manipulation. This lack of confidence can lead to reduced liquidity, increased market volatility, and decreased capital formation, all of which hinder economic growth and stability.

To mitigate the impact of insider trading and uphold market integrity, regulatory bodies and self-regulatory organisations play a crucial role. These entities enforce insider trading laws, monitor trading activities, and investigate suspicious transactions. They aim to detect and prosecute cases of insider trading, impose penalties on violators, and ensure that market participants adhere to ethical and legal standards.

Additionally, organisations and market participants have a responsibility to promote a culture of transparency, disclosure, and compliance. Companies should establish and enforce policies and procedures to prevent insider trading, educate their employees about the legal and ethical implications, and foster a strong ethical culture. Market participants, such as financial institutions and investment professionals, should also prioritise compliance with insider trading regulations, conduct thorough due diligence, and report suspicious activities to regulatory authorities.

Insider trading is considered a serious offence due to its adverse legal and ethical implications. It undermines the principles of fairness, transparency, and equal opportunity in financial markets, distorts market efficiency, and erodes investor confidence. Insider trading laws and regulations aim to deter and punish such practices, emphasising the importance of maintaining the integrity of the capital markets. Upholding ethical standards, promoting transparency, and enforcing regulatory compliance are essential in safeguarding the fairness and trustworthiness of financial markets.

The consequences faced by Martha Stewart

MARTHA STEWART'S CONVICTION and subsequent imprisonment had a significant impact on her personal brand and public perception. As a renowned businesswoman and media personality, Stewart's image was closely tied to her reputation for elegance, style, and domestic expertise. However, the insider trading scandal tarnished her public image and led to various consequences that shaped her personal and professional life.

One of the immediate consequences of Stewart's conviction was the damage to her personal brand. Prior to the scandal, Stewart was synonymous with a lifestyle of refined taste and sophistication. Her name was associated with quality and inspiration in the realms of cooking, homemaking, and entertaining. However, the conviction shattered this carefully cultivated image, as it revealed a breach of trust and integrity. The public perception of Stewart shifted from an admired role model to that of a convicted felon.

Stewart's imprisonment had a profound impact on her personal and professional life. In 2004, she was sentenced to five months in prison, which she served at a federal prison camp in Alderson, West Virginia. The period of incarceration meant not only a physical separation from her family and friends but also a loss of personal freedom and autonomy. This was a significant blow to Stewart, who had built her career and brand around the idea of creating a beautiful and well-curated lifestyle.

From a professional standpoint, Stewart's media empire faced significant challenges during her absence. The scandal affected her company, Martha Stewart Living Omnimedia, as advertisers and sponsors became wary of being associated with a brand tied to criminal activity. The company's stock prices plummeted, and its financial performance suffered. The tarnished reputation of its founder directly impacted the bottom line.

Additionally, Stewart's conviction had an adverse effect on her media presence. Her television show, "Martha Stewart Living," which had been a staple of her brand, experienced a decline in viewership and faced challenges in securing sponsorships. The scandal also led to the cancellation of her spin-off show, "Martha."

Stewart's public image took a hit, and public perception of her changed. She faced scrutiny and criticism from the media and the public, who questioned her ethics and integrity. The insider trading scandal overshadowed her previous achievements and contributions, making it challenging for her to regain public trust and credibility.

However, despite the challenges and negative consequences, Stewart displayed resilience and determination in rebuilding her brand and public image after her release from prison. She actively sought to rehabilitate her reputation and regain the trust of her audience and business partners.

Stewart's comeback strategy involved a combination of efforts to rebuild her brand and personal appearances aimed at humanising her public image. She reestablished her presence in the media by launching new television shows and continuing to publish books and magazines. She emphasised her expertise in the areas of cooking, crafts, and home décor, showcasing her talent and knowledge.

Stewart's ability to bounce back and regain some level of public support was also due to her dedicated fan base and loyal followers. Many individuals admired her skills, creativity, and contributions to the world of homemaking and entertaining. They believed in her ability to provide valuable insights and inspiration, separate from her legal troubles.

Over time, Stewart managed to rebuild her personal brand and revive her media career to some extent. She became involved in various business ventures, including partnerships and collaborations with major companies. She also utilised digital platforms and social media to connect with her audience and promote her brand.

While the impact of Stewart's conviction and imprisonment on her personal brand and public perception cannot be overlooked, it is worth noting that she demonstrated resilience and determination in overcoming the challenges. She was able to leverage her strengths, creativity, and entrepreneurial spirit to rebuild aspects of her career and regain a certain level of success.

Martha Stewart's conviction and imprisonment had a profound impact on her personal brand and public perception. The scandal damaged her reputation, led to financial losses, and affected her media presence. However, Stewart's resilience and efforts to rebuild her brand enabled her to regain some level of success and credibility. The story of her downfall and subsequent comeback serves as a reminder of the consequences of unethical behaviour and the possibilities of redemption in the face of adversity.

What followed?

THE CASE OF INSIDER trading, exemplified by Martha Stewart's involvement, provides us with valuable insights and important lessons about the consequences and ethical implications of such actions. This chapter has shed light on the intricacies of insider trading, the impact it has on the integrity of financial markets, and the repercussions faced by those who engage in this illegal practice.

First and foremost, insider trading serves as a stark reminder of the importance of trust, transparency, and fairness in the world of finance. Financial markets rely on a level playing field where all investors have access to the same information. Any attempt to gain an unfair advantage by trading on non-public material information undermines this fundamental principle. It erodes investor confidence, distorts market efficiency, and creates an atmosphere of inequality and unfairness.

The Martha Stewart case teaches us the gravity of breaching fiduciary duties and the legal and ethical responsibilities that individuals in positions of power hold. Corporate insiders, including executives, directors, and employees, have a duty to act in the best interests of their companies and shareholders. Engaging in insider trading not only violates this duty but also erodes the trust and confidence that shareholders and the public place in these individuals. It highlights the significance of upholding ethical standards and the need for robust governance mechanisms to prevent and detect such misconduct.

Another crucial lesson we can draw from the case is the importance of effective regulation and enforcement. Insider trading laws and regulations are designed to protect investors, maintain market integrity, and ensure a level playing field. Regulatory bodies and self-regulatory organisations play a vital role in monitoring trading activities, investigating suspicious transactions, and prosecuting those who engage in insider trading. It is essential that these entities have the necessary resources, expertise, and authority to effectively enforce the rules and regulations and maintain the integrity of the financial markets.

Additionally, the Martha Stewart case emphasises the need for personal accountability and the consequences of illegal actions. Stewart's conviction and imprisonment serve as a powerful deterrent, illustrating that even prominent individuals can face severe penalties for engaging in insider trading. This serves as a reminder to all market participants that no one is above the law and that the repercussions of illegal activities can be substantial, both in terms of personal and professional consequences.

Furthermore, the Martha Stewart case highlights the importance of reputation and the challenges faced in rebuilding it after a major scandal. Stewart's personal brand suffered a significant blow due to the insider trading scandal. However, her ability to bounce back and regain some level of success demonstrates the power of resilience, determination, and strategic efforts in mitigating the damage caused by unethical behaviour. It serves as a reminder that rebuilding trust and credibility requires consistent ethical conduct, transparency, and genuine efforts to make amends.

Lastly, the case raises broader questions about the ethical responsibilities of individuals and organisations in the business world. It prompts us to reflect on the moral implications of our actions and the impact they have on society. Ethical conduct should not be viewed merely as a legal obligation but as a fundamental principle that guides decision-making and shapes the reputation and legacy of individuals and businesses.

The Martha Stewart case serves as a cautionary tale about the consequences of insider trading and the importance of ethical behaviour in the financial industry. It reminds us of the significance of transparency, fairness, and integrity in maintaining the trust and confidence of investors and the public. By learning from this crime, we can strive to build a financial ecosystem that is characterised by ethical conduct, robust regulation, and a commitment to upholding the principles that underpin our financial markets.

Chapter 3: Money Laundering - The Panama Papers

The Panama Papers represent one of the most significant leaks in the history of investigative journalism, shaking the foundations of the global financial system and exposing the secretive world of offshore finance. The term "Panama Papers" refers to a massive trove of confidential documents that were leaked from the Panamanian law firm Mossack Fonseca in 2016. These leaked documents unveiled a complex network of offshore accounts and shell companies used by individuals and entities to engage in illicit activities such as money laundering, tax evasion, and the concealment of wealth.

The leak of the Panama Papers was an unprecedented event, providing an extraordinary glimpse into the hidden world of offshore finance and exposing the individuals and institutions involved in these secretive practices. The scale of the leak was staggering, with over 11.5 million documents revealing the inner workings of Mossack Fonseca and its clients. The leaked information encompassed a wide range of financial records, emails, contracts, and other sensitive documents, painting a detailed picture of the global offshore industry and its participants.

Mossack Fonseca, a Panama-based law firm founded in 1977, specialised in the creation and administration of offshore companies, providing services that allowed clients to establish entities in tax havens and offshore jurisdictions. The leaked documents disclosed the firm's role in facilitating these activities, offering an unprecedented look at the mechanics of offshore finance and the strategies employed to circumvent legal and regulatory frameworks.

The Panama Papers leak reverberated across the world, captivating the attention of governments, law enforcement agencies, media outlets, and the public. The revelations contained within the documents exposed the involvement of numerous prominent individuals, including politicians, businessmen, celebrities, and public officials from various countries. The leak transcended borders, exposing the global nature of offshore finance and its impact on societies and economies worldwide.

The significance of the Panama Papers lies not only in the vast scale of the leak but also in the profound implications it had for global financial transparency, tax evasion, and illicit financial flows. The leaked documents revealed the extent to which offshore companies and tax havens were utilised as tools to conceal wealth, evade taxes, and engage in illicit activities. They shed light on the mechanisms employed to create complex ownership structures, manipulate transactions, and exploit legal loopholes to the advantage of the wealthy and powerful.

Furthermore, the Panama Papers challenged the notion of financial secrecy and raised serious questions about the integrity of the global financial system. The leak highlighted the role played by offshore jurisdictions in facilitating illicit activities and drew attention to the deficiencies in regulatory oversight and enforcement. It exposed the vulnerabilities and shortcomings that allowed money laundering, tax evasion, and corruption to flourish in the shadows, undermining the fairness and transparency of the global economy.

The Panama Papers also underscored the critical role of investigative journalism and the power of whistleblowers in holding the powerful accountable. The leak was made possible through the collaboration of the International Consortium of Investigative Journalists (ICIJ) and a network of journalists from around the world. Their tireless efforts to analyse and decipher the massive amount of data within the leaked documents resulted in groundbreaking exposés that captured the attention of millions and sparked a global conversation about offshore finance and financial transparency.

The Panama Papers leak represents a watershed moment in the history of financial journalism and global transparency. The leaked documents laid bare the complex web of offshore finance and exposed the extent of illicit activities taking place in the shadows of the global financial system. The revelations within the Panama Papers challenged long-standing assumptions about financial secrecy, prompted calls for regulatory reforms, and highlighted the need for greater transparency and accountability in the world of finance. The impact of the leak continues to reverberate, serving as a catalyst for change and inspiring a global dialogue about the ethical and legal implications of offshore finance.

The significance of the Panama Papers

leak

THE PANAMA PAPERS LEAK, which occurred in 2016, revealed a vast network of offshore accounts and shell companies used for money laundering and tax evasion purposes. The significance of this leak cannot be overstated, as it shed light on the dark underbelly of global financial practices and exposed the scale of illicit activities taking place in the shadows.

The Panama Papers consisted of 11.5 million confidential documents leaked from the Panamanian law firm Mossack Fonseca, a prominent player in the creation and management of offshore companies. These documents exposed the intricate web of financial secrecy and revealed the involvement of numerous individuals, corporations, politicians, and public figures from around the world.

One of the key revelations from the Panama Papers was the extent to which offshore accounts and shell companies were being used to facilitate money laundering and tax evasion. These entities allowed individuals and organisations to hide their wealth, evade taxes, and engage in illicit financial activities with relative ease. The leaked documents provided concrete evidence of the methods used to conceal assets, manipulate transactions, and evade authorities.

The Panama Papers also highlighted the complicity of some offshore jurisdictions in facilitating these illicit practices. Panama, in particular, was known for its lenient regulations and lack of transparency, making it an attractive destination for those seeking to hide their assets and engage in illicit financial activities. The leak exposed the shortcomings in the oversight and regulation of offshore financial centres, leading to increased scrutiny and calls for stronger international cooperation to combat money laundering and tax evasion.

The impact of the Panama Papers leak was far-reaching. It led to investigations, prosecutions, and significant legal and financial consequences for those implicated in the documents. The leak exposed the identities of individuals from various sectors, including politicians, businessmen, celebrities, and public officials. Many faced public outrage, reputational damage, and, in some cases, criminal charges.

Beyond the immediate consequences for individuals involved, the Panama Papers prompted a global conversation about the need for stronger measures to combat financial secrecy and illicit financial flows. The leak exposed the systemic nature of the problem, demonstrating that it was not limited to a few isolated cases but rather a widespread issue with implications for economic development, social equity, and political stability.

The leak also put pressure on governments and international bodies to take action. It led to increased calls for transparency, tax reform, and the implementation of more stringent regulations to prevent money laundering and tax evasion. The revelations in the Panama Papers reinforced the urgency of addressing these issues and the need for international cooperation to tackle them effectively.

Moreover, the leak empowered investigative journalists and whistleblowers, highlighting the crucial role they play in uncovering wrongdoing and holding the powerful accountable. The collaborative efforts of journalists from around the world in analysing and reporting on the leaked documents showcased the potential of investigative journalism to expose complex global financial crimes.

In response to the Panama Papers, some countries took steps to tighten regulations and increase transparency. The Financial Action Task Force (FATF), an intergovernmental body responsible for combating money laundering and terrorist financing, revised its recommendations to address the issues highlighted by the leak. Additionally, governments began sharing information and cooperating more extensively to combat cross-border tax evasion and money laundering.

The significance of the Panama Papers leak lies in its exposure of the dark underbelly of global money laundering and tax evasion. The leaked documents provided unprecedented insight into the scale of illicit financial activities taking place through offshore accounts and shell companies. The revelations prompted global conversations about the need for stronger regulations, transparency, and international cooperation to combat financial secrecy and ensure the integrity of the global financial system. The Panama Papers served as a wake-up call, exposing the vulnerabilities and shortcomings in the regulation of offshore financial centres and calling for comprehensive reforms to address the pervasive issue of money laundering and tax evasion.

The role of offshore accounts and shell companies

OFFSHORE ACCOUNTS AND shell companies play a significant role in facilitating money laundering by providing individuals and entities with a veil of secrecy, allowing them to hide their wealth and evade taxes. These structures enable the movement of illicit funds across borders, making it challenging for authorities to track and trace the origins of the funds. Understanding the mechanics of offshore accounts and shell companies is crucial to comprehending how money laundering takes place.

Offshore accounts are bank accounts held in jurisdictions known as tax havens or offshore financial centres. These jurisdictions typically offer favourable tax regimes, strict bank secrecy laws, and lenient regulations, making them attractive destinations for individuals seeking to hide their assets and evade taxes. Offshore accounts provide a layer of anonymity by using nominee directors or shareholders, ensuring that the true owners of the accounts remain hidden. Additionally, offshore banks often do not cooperate fully with international tax authorities, making it difficult for governments to access information about account holders.

Shell companies, on the other hand, are entities that exist on paper but have no real business operations. They are often established in jurisdictions with lax regulations and weak oversight, making it easy to create and maintain them. Shell companies can be used for legitimate purposes, such as asset protection or confidentiality, but they are also exploited by money launderers. These companies serve as a front, obscuring the true ownership of assets and providing a layer of anonymity to those involved in illicit activities.

The process of money laundering through offshore accounts and shell companies typically involves several steps. The first step is placement, where illicit funds are introduced into the financial system. This could involve depositing cash into an offshore account or investing in assets, such as real estate or luxury goods, through shell companies. By using offshore accounts and shell companies, individuals can distance themselves from the illegal origins of the funds.

The second step is layering, which involves creating complex transactions and moving funds through a series of accounts and transactions to obscure the paper trail. Offshore accounts and shell companies facilitate this process by allowing money launderers to transfer funds between different jurisdictions, making it difficult for authorities to track the movement of the money. Transactions may involve multiple shell companies, making it challenging to identify the ultimate beneficiaries.

The final step is integration, where the laundered funds are reintroduced into the legitimate economy, appearing as clean and legitimate assets. This can be achieved by using offshore accounts to invest in legitimate businesses or by purchasing assets that can be sold or liquidated later. By the time the funds are integrated back into the legitimate economy, their origins are concealed, making it difficult for law enforcement and financial institutions to identify the illicit activities that generated the funds.

Offshore accounts and shell companies also facilitate tax evasion. By placing funds in offshore accounts, individuals can take advantage of favourable tax regimes or exploit the lack of reporting requirements in certain jurisdictions. Offshore accounts allow individuals to keep their assets hidden from their home country's tax authorities, avoiding taxes on income, capital gains, or inheritance. By using shell companies, individuals can also shift profits or manipulate transactions to artificially reduce their tax liabilities.

Moreover, the use of offshore accounts and shell companies can result in significant economic consequences. When individuals evade taxes through these structures, governments lose out on vital tax revenues that could be used for public services, infrastructure development, and social welfare programs. This exacerbates income inequality and hinders economic growth.

Efforts to combat money laundering and tax evasion through offshore accounts and shell companies have been ongoing. International initiatives such as the Common Reporting Standard (CRS) and the Automatic Exchange of Information (AEOI) aim to improve tax transparency by requiring financial institutions to share information about offshore accounts with tax authorities. Governments are also strengthening their anti-money laundering regulations, increasing scrutiny of offshore transactions, and enhancing international cooperation to detect and prevent illicit financial flows.

Offshore accounts and shell companies serve as crucial tools in facilitating money laundering and tax evasion. These structures provide a veil of secrecy, enabling individuals to hide their wealth and obscure the origins of illicit funds. By exploiting favourable tax regimes, lax regulations, and strict bank secrecy laws, money launderers can move funds across borders and integrate them back into the legitimate economy, making it challenging for authorities to detect and prevent these illicit activities. Efforts to combat money laundering and tax evasion through offshore accounts and shell companies are necessary to safeguard the integrity of the global financial system and ensure that individuals and entities are held accountable for their financial activities.

The impact of the Panama Papers on international politics and regulatory efforts

THE RELEASE OF THE Panama Papers in 2016 had a significant impact on international politics and regulatory efforts, sparking widespread calls for reform and raising awareness about the need to combat money laundering and tax evasion. The leaked documents exposed the extent of global financial secrecy, implicating prominent individuals and institutions from around the world. In response to this exposé, various reforms were initiated to enhance transparency, strengthen regulations, and improve international cooperation. However, the effectiveness of these reforms in combating money laundering remains a subject of ongoing debate.

One of the immediate consequences of the Panama Papers was the increased scrutiny on tax havens and offshore financial centres. The leak shed light on the role of these jurisdictions in facilitating illicit financial activities and evading taxes. It prompted governments and international organisations to take action to address these issues. The Organization for Economic Cooperation and Development (OECD) launched the Common Reporting Standard (CRS), which aims to improve tax transparency by requiring financial institutions to share information about offshore accounts with tax authorities. Over 100 countries have committed to implementing the CRS, facilitating the exchange of financial information and enhancing efforts to combat tax evasion.

Furthermore, the Financial Action Task Force (FATF), an intergovernmental body that sets standards for combating money laundering and terrorist financing, issued recommendations to strengthen anti-money laundering (AML) regulations and enhance the transparency of beneficial ownership. These recommendations encourage countries to improve their legal frameworks, conduct risk assessments, and establish mechanisms to identify the ultimate beneficiaries of companies and trusts. The Panama Papers brought attention to the vulnerabilities in beneficial ownership regulations and the role they play in facilitating illicit activities, leading to a push for reforms in this area.

Some countries responded to the Panama Papers by introducing legislative changes and stricter regulatory measures. For example, the European Union (EU) implemented the Fifth Anti-Money Laundering Directive (5AMLD) in 2018, which requires member states to maintain registers of beneficial ownership and cooperate more effectively in sharing information. The directive aims to improve the detection and prevention of money laundering and enhance transparency in financial transactions.

Additionally, some jurisdictions named in the Panama Papers faced pressure to reform their practices. Panama itself, where the law firm Mossack Fonseca was based, took steps to improve its regulatory framework and enhance cooperation with international authorities. The country introduced new laws to enhance due diligence requirements, implemented stricter rules for the registration and operation of companies, and bolstered its regulatory oversight. Other offshore jurisdictions, such as the British Virgin Islands, also faced calls for reforms and implemented measures to enhance transparency and combat money laundering.

While these regulatory efforts and reforms are steps in the right direction, their effectiveness in combating money laundering remains a matter of ongoing evaluation. Critics argue that the reforms may not be sufficient to address the systemic issues exposed by the Panama Papers. They argue that stronger enforcement mechanisms and international cooperation are necessary to ensure compliance and hold individuals and entities accountable for their involvement in illicit financial activities.

One challenge in combating money laundering is the complex and constantly evolving nature of illicit finance. Money launderers adapt their methods to exploit loopholes and weaknesses in the system. The use of offshore accounts and shell companies continues to evolve, and new techniques emerge to conceal the origins of illicit funds. Regulatory efforts must keep pace with these developments to effectively combat money laundering.

International cooperation is also crucial in combating money laundering, as illicit funds often flow across borders. The Panama Papers highlighted the need for improved cooperation and information sharing among countries. While progress has been made in this regard, there is still room for improvement. Enhanced collaboration among governments, financial institutions, and law enforcement agencies is necessary to detect and prevent money laundering effectively.

The Panama Papers had a profound impact on international politics and regulatory efforts. The exposé led to reforms aimed at enhancing transparency, strengthening regulations, and improving international cooperation. The introduction of initiatives such as the Common Reporting Standard and the Fifth Anti-Money Laundering Directive are positive steps toward combating money laundering and tax evasion. However, the effectiveness of these reforms remains an ongoing challenge. Continued efforts to improve regulations, enhance international cooperation, and adapt to evolving money laundering techniques are necessary to effectively combat illicit financial activities and ensure the integrity of the global financial system.

What followed?

THE ISSUE OF MONEY laundering is a pervasive and complex problem that poses significant threats to the integrity of the global financial system. The exploration of money laundering, its techniques, and its consequences through the lens of the Panama Papers has provided valuable insights and important learnings. As we conclude this chapter, it is crucial to reflect on these learnings and consider the implications for combating money laundering effectively.

First and foremost, the Panama Papers shed light on the extent and magnitude of money laundering and tax evasion facilitated by offshore accounts and shell companies. The leaked documents exposed the dark underbelly of global financial secrecy, revealing the widespread use of these structures to hide wealth, evade taxes, and launder illicit funds. This knowledge reinforces the need for robust regulatory frameworks and international cooperation to prevent and detect these illicit activities.

One of the key learnings from the Panama Papers is the critical importance of transparency and beneficial ownership disclosure. The use of nominee directors and complex ownership structures obscures the true beneficiaries of offshore accounts and shell companies, making it difficult for authorities to identify those involved in money laundering. Requiring comprehensive and accurate information on beneficial ownership can be a powerful tool in combating money laundering, as it enhances transparency, accountability, and the ability to trace illicit funds.

Moreover, the Panama Papers underscored the significance of international cooperation in addressing money laundering. The cross-border nature of illicit financial flows demands collaboration among countries, financial institutions, and law enforcement agencies. The leaks revealed how money launderers exploit loopholes and jurisdictional differences to move funds seamlessly across borders. To effectively combat money laundering, robust mechanisms for information sharing, mutual legal assistance, and coordinated investigations are essential.

Another critical learning is the need for stringent regulatory oversight and enforcement. The Panama Papers exposed weaknesses in regulatory frameworks that allowed money laundering to flourish. To effectively combat this crime, regulations must be robust, comprehensive, and adaptable to changing tactics employed by money launderers. Governments and regulatory bodies must allocate adequate resources to monitor compliance, conduct thorough investigations, and impose appropriate penalties on those involved in money laundering activities.

Additionally, technology and data analysis play a crucial role in detecting and preventing money laundering. The sheer volume of financial transactions and the complexity of illicit networks make it impractical to rely solely on manual investigation methods. Advanced analytical tools and artificial intelligence can aid in identifying suspicious patterns, anomalies, and connections that may indicate potential money laundering activities. Embracing technological advancements can significantly enhance the effectiveness and efficiency of anti-money laundering efforts.

Furthermore, the Panama Papers exposed the inherent risks associated with offshore financial centres and tax havens. While these jurisdictions may offer legitimate services and attract legitimate investments, they are also susceptible to abuse by money launderers and tax evaders. Governments and international bodies must work together to establish higher standards for these jurisdictions, promote transparency, and discourage the misuse of offshore accounts and shell companies.

Lastly, public awareness and accountability are crucial in the fight against money laundering. The Panama Papers generated significant public interest and outrage, emphasising the need for public pressure to drive reforms and hold individuals and institutions accountable for their involvement in illicit financial activities. It is essential to foster a culture of integrity, transparency, and responsible financial behaviour to create an environment where money laundering is less likely to thrive.

The Panama Papers have provided invaluable lessons in understanding the complexities and consequences of money laundering. The exploration of offshore accounts, shell companies, and the global network of illicit financial flows has highlighted the urgent need for comprehensive reforms, transparency, international cooperation, and robust enforcement mechanisms. By learning from these insights, we can strengthen our collective efforts to combat money laundering, protect the integrity of the financial system, and promote a fair and transparent global economy.

UNVEILING THE SHADOWS: A JOURNEY INTO FINANCIAL CRIMES AND SCANDALS

Chapter 4: Tax Evasion - Lionel Messi

Lionel Messi, often referred to as one of the greatest football players of all time, is an Argentine professional footballer who has captivated the world with his extraordinary talent, unparalleled skills, and remarkable achievements. Born on June 24, 1987, in Rosario, Argentina, Messi's journey from a young boy with a passion for football to a global sporting icon is an inspiring tale of perseverance, dedication, and unmatched talent.

From a young age, Messi showcased exceptional footballing abilities that set him apart from his peers. His talent was evident even as a child, and he quickly caught the attention of scouts from prestigious football clubs. At the tender age of 13, Messi left his hometown to join the renowned FC Barcelona's youth academy, La Masia, in Spain, where he honed his skills and developed into the prodigious player he is today.

Messi's rise to prominence in the world of football was meteoric. Making his debut for FC Barcelona's first team in 2004 at the age of 17, he swiftly became an integral part of the squad and an emblematic figure for the club. Known for his exceptional dribbling skills, precise passing, lightning speed, and incredible goal-scoring ability, Messi quickly established himself as a force to be reckoned with on the football pitch.

Over the years, Messi's list of accolades and records has grown exponentially. He has won numerous individual awards, including the prestigious FIFA Ballon d'Or, which he has won multiple times, cementing his status as one of the greatest players in the history of the sport. Messi's ability to consistently perform at an extraordinary level, year after year, has set him apart from his contemporaries and earned him the admiration and respect of football fans worldwide.

One of Messi's most remarkable achievements is his extraordinary goal-scoring prowess. He has broken countless records, including becoming FC Barcelona's all-time top scorer, surpassing the legendary record set by the club's previous goal-scoring maestro, César Rodríguez. Messi's ability to score goals with remarkable precision, whether from close range or from long-range strikes, has mesmerised audiences and earned him the reputation of being a true goal-scoring phenomenon.

In addition to his club success, Messi has also been a key figure for the Argentine national team. Representing his country in various international competitions, including the FIFA World Cup and the Copa America, Messi has displayed his immense talent on the global stage. While success at the international level has eluded him, his impact on the team and his commitment to representing Argentina have never wavered.

Off the field, Messi is known for his humble demeanour, soft-spoken nature, and dedication to his craft. He has become an inspirational figure for aspiring footballers worldwide, serving as a role model for determination, hard work, and sportsmanship. Despite his immense success and global fame, Messi has remained grounded and committed to giving back to society. He has established charitable foundations and initiatives, using his platform and resources to make a positive impact on the lives of others.

Lionel Messi's journey from a young boy in Rosario, Argentina, to becoming one of the greatest football players the world has ever seen is a testament to his exceptional talent, unwavering dedication, and unrivalled passion for the beautiful game. His achievements, records, and impact on the sport have solidified his place in football history. Messi's remarkable skills, humble personality, and inspiring story continue to captivate football fans, making him an icon both on and off the field.

The Lionel Messi tax evasion case

THE LIONEL MESSI TAX evasion case sent shockwaves through the world of football and brought into question the financial practices of one of the sport's biggest stars. The case involved allegations of tax fraud against Messi and his father, Jorge Messi, relating to their management of the player's image rights. The accusations centred on their alleged attempts to avoid paying taxes on the substantial income generated from these rights. This chapter will delve into the key allegations against Messi and his father, as well as the methods they purportedly used to evade taxes.

The allegations against Lionel Messi and his father stemmed from their handling of the player's image rights, which are often a significant source of income for high-profile athletes. The

Spanish tax authorities claimed that between 2007 and 2009, Messi and his father created a complex web of offshore companies in tax havens such as Belize and Uruguay to channel income from image rights, thereby avoiding tax obligations in Spain.

The prosecution argued that the Messis utilised these offshore entities to make it appear as though the income derived from image rights belonged to these companies rather than the players themselves. By doing so, they allegedly avoided declaring this income in Spain and consequently evaded paying the corresponding taxes. It was alleged that Messi's father, Jorge, took the lead in managing these financial arrangements.

The prosecution contended that the Messis' actions constituted a deliberate and coordinated effort to defraud the Spanish tax authorities. They argued that the offshore companies were mere fronts designed to conceal the true nature of the income and avoid tax liabilities. The prosecutor maintained that Messi and his father had knowledge of the scheme and actively participated in its implementation.

Throughout the trial, the defence argued that Messi was unaware of the financial arrangements and that his father handled all matters related to his finances. They claimed that Lionel Messi focused solely on his football career and trusted his father to manage his financial affairs, including the handling of image rights. The defence portrayed Messi as an innocent party, emphasising his lack of involvement in the intricate details of the family's financial operations.

The defence further asserted that any irregularities or omissions in tax declarations were not intentional but rather the result of poor financial advice from external consultants and professionals hired by Messi's father. They contended that Messi relied on these experts and trusted their guidance, placing the blame on them for any wrongdoing.

However, the court rejected the defence's arguments and found both Lionel Messi and his father guilty of tax evasion. In July 2016, Messi was sentenced to 21 months in prison, while his father received a slightly longer sentence of 21 months and 15 days. Nonetheless, it is important to note that in Spain, prison sentences of fewer than two years for non-violent offences are typically suspended for first-time offenders. As a result, neither Messi nor his father served time in prison.

The Lionel Messi tax evasion case generated widespread media attention and ignited debates surrounding the responsibility of high-profile individuals to fulfil their tax obligations. It raised questions about the use of offshore companies and tax havens to shield income from taxation, highlighting the potential abuses and loopholes in the international tax system.

The case also emphasised the importance of proper financial management, accountability, and transparency, particularly for individuals with substantial wealth and income. It served as a reminder that even those who are seemingly removed from financial matters should remain vigilant and informed about their financial affairs to ensure compliance with tax regulations.

Furthermore, the Messi case prompted calls for greater scrutiny and regulation in the realm of image rights and their taxation. The complexity of these arrangements and the potential for abuse necessitate enhanced oversight and clearer guidelines to prevent similar cases of tax evasion in the future.

The Lionel Messi tax evasion case involved allegations of using offshore entities to evade taxes on income derived from image rights. The prosecution claimed that Messi and his father were complicit in creating a complex web of offshore companies to hide income and avoid tax obligations. Despite the defence's arguments of Messi's limited involvement and reliance on his father and external advisors, the court found both Messi and his father guilty of tax evasion. The case shed light on the importance of proper financial management, transparency, and accountability for high-profile individuals and highlighted the need for stronger regulation and oversight in the realm of image rights taxation.

The issue of tax evasion in professional sports

TAX EVASION IN PROFESSIONAL sports has become a prevalent problem that has garnered significant attention in recent years. This issue arises from various factors, including the complex nature of athletes' income, international transfers, and the use of offshore structures. The allure of significant financial gain, coupled with the potential loopholes in tax systems, has created an environment conducive to tax evasion. To combat this problem, authorities, sports organisations, and governments have started implementing measures to increase transparency, strengthen regulations, and enhance cooperation between jurisdictions.

One of the reasons tax evasion has become a prevalent issue in professional sports is the intricate structure of athletes' income. High-profile athletes often earn substantial amounts of money from various sources, including salaries, bonuses, endorsements, and image rights. These income streams can be subject to different tax regulations and rates, creating opportunities for individuals to exploit discrepancies and avoid paying their fair share of taxes. Athletes and their advisors may seek to take advantage of complex financial arrangements to reduce their tax liabilities, including the use of offshore entities, royalty payments, and licensing agreements.

International transfers of athletes further complicate the tax landscape. When players move from one country to another, they may face tax obligations in both their home country and the destination country. This dual tax liability can create opportunities for tax planning and potentially result in the manipulation of income and expenses to minimise tax payments. The lack of harmonised regulations and coordination between countries exacerbates the challenges in enforcing tax compliance and combating evasion in the realm of international sports.

The use of offshore structures and tax havens is another significant factor contributing to tax evasion in professional sports. Offshore entities provide individuals with opportunities to shield their income, assets, and transactions from scrutiny and taxation. By establishing companies in jurisdictions with favourable tax regimes and strict banking secrecy laws, athletes can potentially hide income and avoid tax obligations. The opacity and complexity of offshore structures make it difficult for tax authorities to detect and combat tax evasion effectively.

In response to the prevalent issue of tax evasion in professional sports, various measures are being taken to address the problem. Governments and tax authorities have been strengthening regulations and increasing scrutiny on high-income earners, including athletes. They are focusing on improving transparency, closing loopholes, and ensuring that tax regulations keep pace with the evolving landscape of sports and financial practices.

One key measure is the implementation of stricter reporting requirements. Tax authorities are demanding more comprehensive and detailed disclosure of athletes' income, including image rights and endorsement deals. By requiring transparent reporting, authorities aim to reduce the opportunity for athletes to underreport or hide income, making tax evasion more difficult to carry out.

Furthermore, there is an increasing emphasis on international cooperation and information exchange between tax jurisdictions. Countries are working together to share financial information, track cross-border transactions, and identify potential tax evaders. Initiatives such as the Common Reporting Standard (CRS) and Automatic Exchange of Information (AEOI) facilitate the exchange of financial data between countries, making it harder for individuals to hide income and assets offshore.

Sports organisations themselves are also taking steps to address tax evasion within their industry. For instance, some leagues and governing bodies are implementing stricter regulations and codes of conduct to ensure that athletes fulfil their tax obligations. These organisations are raising awareness among athletes and providing guidance on tax compliance, encouraging them to engage in responsible financial management and seek reputable advisors who adhere to ethical practices.

Additionally, increased public scrutiny and media attention on tax evasion cases involving high-profile athletes have brought this issue to the forefront. The public and fans are demanding greater accountability and integrity from sports stars, putting pressure on athletes to maintain a strong ethical stance and fulfil their tax responsibilities.

Tax evasion in professional sports has become a prevalent problem due to factors such as the complex nature of athletes' income, international transfers, and the use of offshore structures. To address this issue, measures are being taken at various levels. Governments are strengthening regulations and improving international cooperation to increase transparency and detect tax evasion. Sports organisations are implementing stricter codes of conduct, and there is growing public awareness and demand for greater accountability. By addressing the root causes and implementing comprehensive measures, authorities and stakeholders aim to combat tax evasion in professional sports and ensure a fair and transparent financial environment for athletes and the industry as a whole.

The legal consequences faced by Messi and his father

THE LEGAL CONSEQUENCES faced by Lionel Messi and his father in the tax evasion case had a significant impact on both Messi's personal reputation and his standing in the football world. As one of the greatest football players of his generation and a global icon, Messi's involvement in such a high-profile legal battle attracted widespread attention and scrutiny. This chapter will explore how the case affected Messi's reputation, his relationship with fans and sponsors, and his overall standing within the football community.

Prior to the tax evasion case, Lionel Messi had cultivated a positive public image as a humble and talented footballer. He was widely regarded as a role model for aspiring players and had amassed a massive following of fans around the world. However, the revelations and subsequent legal proceedings tarnished this image and led to a significant dent in his reputation.

The tax evasion case brought to light allegations that Messi and his father had attempted to avoid paying taxes on substantial income from image rights through the use of offshore companies. While Messi and his defence team maintained his innocence and claimed he was unaware of the financial intricacies involved, the court found him guilty of the charges. The conviction reinforced the perception that Messi, despite his on-field prowess, was entangled in questionable financial practices.

The impact of the case on Messi's reputation was felt both within and outside the football community. Some fans remained loyal and supportive of their idol, believing in his innocence or empathising with the complexities of managing his finances. However, others were disillusioned and felt betrayed by the fact that their footballing hero had been involved in an illegal financial scheme. The case created a division among fans, with some continuing to idolise Messi for his on-field brilliance while others questioned his integrity off the pitch.

From a commercial perspective, Messi's sponsorship deals also came under scrutiny in the wake of the tax evasion case. Sponsors, who are typically cautious about being associated with individuals involved in legal controversies, closely monitored the situation. While some sponsors remained loyal and continued their partnerships with Messi, others chose to distance themselves, fearing potential damage to their brand image. The case became a public relations challenge for both Messi and his sponsors, requiring careful management and communication to mitigate the negative impact.

In terms of Messi's standing within the football world, the tax evasion case did not diminish his exceptional skills as a player. He continued to excel on the pitch, breaking records and winning trophies. However, the case did cast a shadow over his achievements, with critics using it as an opportunity to question the integrity of his success. Some argued that Messi's sporting excellence was tainted by the association with tax evasion, undermining his status as a role model and ambassador for the sport.

The case also sparked discussions about the responsibility of athletes and their role in society. As highly influential figures, athletes are often expected to uphold moral and ethical standards. The tax evasion case challenged this perception and raised questions about the accountability of sports stars for their financial actions. The incident served as a reminder that talent and success in sports do not exempt individuals from legal and ethical obligations.

Despite the negative impact on Messi's reputation, he has taken steps to rebuild trust and repair the damage caused by the case. In the aftermath of the legal proceedings, Messi and his legal team paid the outstanding taxes and associated fines, demonstrating a willingness to rectify the situation. He also made efforts to communicate with his fans and the public, expressing regret for the incident and emphasising his commitment to comply with tax regulations in the future.

Over time, Messi's performance on the pitch and continued success have played a significant role in restoring his standing within the football world. His exceptional skills and consistent excellence have allowed many fans to separate his sporting achievements from the controversy surrounding the tax evasion case. Messi's continued success has helped shift the focus back to his footballing prowess, reminding the world of his incredible talent and allowing him to regain some of the respect and admiration he enjoyed prior to the case.

The legal consequences faced by Lionel Messi and his father in the tax evasion case had a substantial impact on Messi's personal reputation and his standing in the football world. The case led to a division among fans, affected his sponsorship deals, and raised questions about his integrity and accountability. However, Messi's continued success on the pitch and his efforts to rectify the situation have played a role in restoring his standing and reminding the world of his exceptional footballing talent.

What followed?

THE CASE OF TAX EVASION involving Lionel Messi and his father highlights the significant consequences and broader lessons associated with this crime. As we conclude this chapter, it is important to reflect on the key learnings that can be drawn from this case and the implications for individuals, society, and the sports industry as a whole.

First and foremost, the Messi tax evasion case serves as a stark reminder that tax evasion is a serious offence with severe legal and reputational consequences. Regardless of an individual's status, wealth, or accomplishments, everyone is obligated to fulfil their tax responsibilities. The case underscores the importance of transparency, accountability, and adherence to tax regulations, regardless of one's occupation or financial situation.

One of the crucial lessons from this case is the necessity for individuals to have a clear understanding of their financial affairs. Messi's defence argued that he relied on his father and advisors for the management of his finances, but ultimately, it is essential for individuals to take an active role in understanding their financial transactions and tax obligations. Being aware of one's financial activities and seeking professional advice from reputable experts can help prevent unintentional involvement in unlawful practices.

The Messi case also highlights the importance of robust financial regulations and oversight. Governments and regulatory bodies need to ensure that tax laws are clear, enforceable, and capable of addressing the complexities of modern financial practices. There is a need for continuous evaluation and refinement of regulations to keep pace with evolving financial structures and international transactions.

Furthermore, the case emphasises the significance of international cooperation in combating tax evasion. As athletes and high-net-worth individuals often engage in cross-border financial activities, collaboration between jurisdictions becomes crucial to detect and prevent tax evasion effectively. The exchange of financial information, as seen in initiatives like the Common Reporting Standard (CRS) and Automatic Exchange of Information (AEOI), plays a pivotal role in detecting hidden assets and unreported income.

The Messi tax evasion case has broader implications for the sports industry. It underscores the responsibility of athletes as role models and ambassadors for the sport. Athletes, particularly those in the public eye, have a duty to maintain high ethical standards, not only on the field but also in their financial affairs. This case serves as a reminder that fame and success do not exempt individuals from legal and ethical obligations.

Sports organisations, governing bodies, and sponsors have an important role to play in preventing tax evasion and promoting financial integrity. Strict codes of conduct, comprehensive education programs, and increased scrutiny can help ensure that athletes understand their obligations and the potential consequences of engaging in unlawful financial practices. Sponsors should also carefully consider the reputation and integrity of individuals before entering into endorsement deals.

For individuals and society, the Messi tax evasion case highlights the significance of fair taxation. When high-profile individuals evade taxes, it places an increased burden on ordinary citizens and undermines public trust in the tax system. The case serves as a reminder that tax revenues play a vital role in funding essential public services and infrastructure. Ensuring that everyone pays their fair share of taxes is crucial for social and economic development.

The Lionel Messi tax evasion case offers valuable insights and lessons for individuals, society, and the sports industry. It highlights the seriousness of tax evasion, the importance of personal financial awareness, and the need for robust regulations and international cooperation. Athletes and high-profile individuals have a responsibility to uphold ethical standards, and sports organisations and sponsors must promote financial integrity. Ultimately, the case reminds us that fair and transparent taxation is vital for the well-being of society as a whole.

Chapter 5: Elite Sex Trafficking and Exploitation - Jeffrey Epstein

Jeffrey Epstein was a wealthy financier who became notorious for his involvement in a high-profile sex trafficking scandal. Born on January 20, 1953, in Brooklyn, New York, Epstein led a life shrouded in mystery and controversy until his arrest in 2019. His rise to prominence in the financial world, his connections to influential individuals, and the heinous crimes he perpetrated have captivated public attention and raised significant questions about power, privilege, and the abuse of vulnerable individuals.

Epstein began his career in finance, working for prominent investment banks such as Bear Stearns and later establishing his own firm, J. Epstein & Co. His exact sources of wealth remain a subject of speculation, but he cultivated relationships with influential figures in various industries, including politics, academia, and entertainment. His connections allowed him to move within elite social circles and gain access to the highest echelons of society.

It was in this context of influence and affluence that Epstein's dark activities took place. In 2005, he faced accusations of sexual abuse involving underage girls, and an extensive investigation into his illicit activities was launched. However, a controversial plea deal in 2008 resulted in a lenient sentence, with Epstein serving just 13 months in a county jail, primarily on work release. The deal drew widespread criticism, raising concerns about the preferential treatment of the wealthy and well-connected.

Epstein's crimes continued to surface, and in 2019, he was arrested again on federal charges of sex trafficking of minors. The case attracted intense media scrutiny, as it unravelled a complex web of exploitation, manipulation, and abuse. It was alleged that Epstein had established a vast network of underage victims whom he exploited for his own gratification and facilitated the involvement of influential individuals in his activities.

The shocking revelations surrounding Epstein's sex trafficking ring sent shockwaves throughout the world. The scope of the scandal, coupled with the involvement of high-profile individuals, prompted widespread public outrage and demands for accountability. The case raised profound questions about the abuse of power, the vulnerability of marginalised individuals, and the extent to which the wealthy and influential can evade justice.

Epstein's arrest marked the beginning of a legal battle that would never reach its conclusion. While in custody, awaiting trial, Epstein was found dead in his jail cell in August 2019. His death was officially ruled as suicide, although it has been subject to intense speculation and conspiracy theories.

The Epstein case has had far-reaching implications, extending beyond the individual himself. It has exposed the dark underbelly of elite sex trafficking and exploitation, revealing the extent to which powerful individuals can manipulate and exploit vulnerable victims. The scandal has ignited discussions about the protection of victims, the role of enablers, and the failures of the criminal justice system to hold the powerful accountable.

Jeffrey Epstein's life and actions have left an indelible mark on the public consciousness. From his rise to prominence in the financial world to his involvement in a sex trafficking scandal, his story represents a disturbing intersection of wealth, power, and abuse. The Epstein case serves as a powerful reminder of the need for justice, transparency, and the protection of the most vulnerable members of society.

The life and actions of Jeffrey Epstein

JEFFREY EPSTEIN'S LIFE and actions reveal a disturbing pattern of manipulation, abuse, and exploitation. To fully understand the extent of his crimes, it is necessary to delve into his network-building strategies and the methods he employed to engage in sex trafficking and exploitation.

Epstein's network-building began early in his career as a financier. His exact sources of wealth remain a subject of speculation, but he managed to establish connections with influential individuals from various industries, including politics, academia, and entertainment. Epstein's association with prestigious institutions like Harvard University and his philanthropic endeavours helped him forge relationships with prominent figures, enabling him to move within elite social circles.

One key factor in Epstein's network-building was his ability to exploit his connections for personal gain. He portrayed himself as a well-connected and wealthy individual, offering access to influential people and exclusive opportunities. Through this facade, Epstein enticed individuals into his orbit, creating a web of relationships that he would later leverage to facilitate his criminal activities.

Epstein's method of sex trafficking and exploitation involved the recruitment and grooming of underage girls. He strategically targeted vulnerable individuals from disadvantaged backgrounds, often luring them with promises of financial assistance, educational opportunities, or modelling careers. Epstein and his associates, including his longtime confidante Ghislaine Maxwell, would use manipulation, coercion, and financial incentives to control and exploit these young victims.

Once ensnared in his network, Epstein would subject his victims to a cycle of abuse. He would allegedly engage in sexual acts with them himself, while also coercing them into sexual encounters with other powerful individuals within his network. By exploiting his victims' vulnerabilities, Epstein exerted control over them and created an environment of fear and dependency.

Epstein's network was not limited to his own actions but extended to the participation of influential individuals. The case revealed a web of powerful figures from various industries who allegedly engaged in sexual acts with underage girls procured by Epstein. The exact extent of their involvement and the identities of all the individuals implicated are still subjects of investigation and legal proceedings.

Epstein's ability to maintain secrecy and avoid detection for an extended period is indicative of the complexity and depth of his network. Reports suggest that he went to great lengths to protect his activities, employing sophisticated methods to evade scrutiny. These included the use of private jets, luxurious properties, and encrypted communication systems. Epstein's wealth and influence afforded him a certain level of protection, shielding him from the consequences of his actions for many years.

It is important to recognize that the Epstein case not only exposes the actions of an individual but also reveals systemic failures. The case raises questions about the accountability of powerful individuals, the protection of vulnerable victims, and the effectiveness of law enforcement and regulatory institutions in combating such crimes. The ability of Epstein to operate with relative impunity for a significant period underscores the need for improved protocols, investigative mechanisms, and legal frameworks to prevent and address cases of sex trafficking and exploitation.

Jeffrey Epstein's network-building strategies and methods of engaging in sex trafficking and exploitation reveal a deeply disturbing pattern of abuse and manipulation. Through his connections, he created a web of influence that enabled him to prey on vulnerable young girls and involve powerful individuals in his criminal activities. The case underscores the urgent need for robust mechanisms to protect victims, hold perpetrators accountable, and prevent such heinous crimes from occurring in the future.

The involvement of influential individuals in Epstein's activities

THE INVOLVEMENT OF influential individuals in Jeffrey Epstein's activities has been a significant aspect of the scandal surrounding his sex trafficking and exploitation ring. The case has revealed a disturbing network of powerful figures from various industries who were alleged to have participated in Epstein's crimes. While the full extent of their involvement is still a subject of investigation and legal proceedings, several notable figures have been associated with Epstein, raising profound implications for their reputations and the broader issues of accountability and justice.

One of the most prominent figures associated with Epstein is Prince Andrew, Duke of York, and a member of the British royal family. Epstein and Prince Andrew developed a friendship in the 1990s, and their relationship came under intense scrutiny when Epstein was first investigated for sexual abuse in 2005. Allegations emerged that Prince Andrew had engaged in sexual activities with an underage girl who was reportedly trafficked by Epstein. Despite denying the accusations, Prince Andrew's association with Epstein has had a profound impact on his public image, leading to his withdrawal from official royal duties.

Another influential figure connected to Epstein is former President Bill Clinton. Clinton's relationship with Epstein was a subject of controversy, as flight logs revealed that Clinton had flown on Epstein's private jet, dubbed the "Lolita Express," multiple times. However, Clinton denied any knowledge of Epstein's criminal activities and stated that he had not visited Epstein's private island or had a close personal relationship with him. Nevertheless, the association with Epstein has tarnished Clinton's reputation and raised questions about the judgement and associations of a former U.S. president.

Renowned scientist and author, Stephen Hawking, was also linked to Epstein. It was reported that Epstein had sponsored a conference on the island of St. Thomas, where Hawking attended and gave a lecture. However, there is no evidence to suggest that Hawking was involved in any of Epstein's criminal activities. The association, nonetheless, highlighted the diverse range of influential individuals who had crossed paths with Epstein.

Other notable figures associated with Epstein include Prince Albert II of Monaco, former Israeli Prime Minister Ehud Barak, and prominent lawyers, academics, and business moguls. The involvement of these individuals, if proven, carries significant implications for their public image and reputation. It exposes the potential complicity or at least association with a convicted sex offender engaged in the exploitation of vulnerable individuals.

The implications of the alleged participation of these influential figures extend beyond individual reputations. They raise questions about the abuse of power, the vulnerability of victims, and the challenges in holding powerful individuals accountable. The Epstein case highlights the potential for manipulation and the influence that wealthy and well-connected individuals can wield to evade justice and perpetrate heinous crimes.

Furthermore, the association of influential individuals with Epstein underscores the need for thorough investigations and the importance of ensuring that justice is served without bias or favouritism. It is crucial to determine the extent of involvement and the level of accountability for each individual implicated in Epstein's activities, while also addressing any systemic failures that may have enabled his criminal conduct to persist.

The alleged participation of influential individuals in Epstein's activities also serves as a wake-up call for societies to reevaluate the structures that enable such abuse to occur. It emphasises the need for robust legal frameworks, enhanced protections for victims, and a commitment to holding individuals accountable regardless of their status or connections.

The involvement of influential individuals in Jeffrey Epstein's activities has had far-reaching implications. The association with Epstein has damaged reputations and raised questions about accountability, power dynamics, and the protection of vulnerable individuals. It is essential that thorough investigations take place to determine the extent of involvement and to ensure that justice is served. The Epstein case serves as a stark reminder of the potential for abuse and manipulation by those in positions of power and influence, highlighting the urgent need for systemic reforms to prevent and address such heinous crimes in the future.

The legal aftermath of Epstein's arrest and death

THE LEGAL AFTERMATH of Jeffrey Epstein's arrest and subsequent death has had significant implications for the victims, the public perception of the justice system, and ongoing investigations. The circumstances surrounding Epstein's case, including the lenient plea deal he received in 2008 and his mysterious death in jail, have fueled widespread outrage and cast doubt on the integrity of the legal proceedings.

One of the immediate impacts of Epstein's arrest was the reopening of the case and the opportunity for his victims to seek justice. Epstein's victims, who had long been denied their day in court, finally had an opportunity to share their stories and confront their abuser. The case shed light on the horrific experiences these individuals had endured and brought attention to the broader issue of sex trafficking and exploitation. The legal proceedings provided an avenue for the victims to be heard and played a crucial role in validating their experiences.

However, the circumstances surrounding Epstein's death in jail in August 2019 raised serious questions about the handling of the case and the transparency of the justice system. Epstein's death, ruled as suicide by hanging, occurred while he was in federal custody, awaiting trial on charges of sex trafficking and conspiracy. The incident sparked widespread speculation and conspiracy theories, with many questioning the official explanation and alleging foul play. The circumstances surrounding his death fueled public distrust and eroded confidence in the ability of the justice system to hold powerful individuals accountable.

Epstein's death also had profound implications for ongoing investigations and the pursuit of justice. With his death, the criminal case against him was effectively terminated, preventing a full trial that could have brought to light more evidence and potentially implicated additional individuals. The abrupt end to the legal proceedings left many unanswered questions and denied the victims the opportunity for a comprehensive legal resolution.

Moreover, Epstein's death highlighted institutional failures and the need for a thorough examination of the circumstances leading to his demise. The incident prompted inquiries into the management of the correctional facility where he was held, raising concerns about negligence, lack of proper supervision, and potential misconduct by prison staff. The questions surrounding Epstein's death and the subsequent investigations have further undermined public confidence in the justice system and fueled scepticism about its ability to handle high-profile cases with transparency and fairness.

The legal aftermath of Epstein's case also led to increased scrutiny of the plea deal he received in 2008, which allowed him to plead guilty to lesser state charges of solicitation of prostitution and serve a minimal sentence. The lenient agreement, negotiated by then-U.S. Attorney Alexander Acosta, came under intense criticism for its failure to adequately address the severity of Epstein's crimes and provide justice for the victims. The controversy surrounding the plea deal eventually led to Acosta's resignation as U.S. Secretary of Labor in 2019.

The fallout from Epstein's case has also prompted broader investigations into the potential involvement of other influential individuals in his sex trafficking and exploitation network. Prosecutors have continued to pursue charges against Epstein's alleged accomplices, including his longtime associate Ghislaine Maxwell. Maxwell was arrested in 2020 and faces multiple charges, including sex trafficking of minors and perjury. Her trial, which is scheduled for later in 2021, is expected to shed further light on the extent of Epstein's operations and potentially implicate other individuals.

The legal aftermath of Epstein's arrest and death has left a profound impact on the victims, the public perception of the justice system, and ongoing investigations. The case has exposed institutional failures, raised questions about accountability, and highlighted the challenges of pursuing justice in cases involving powerful individuals. It has underscored the need for comprehensive reforms to ensure the protection of victims, the transparency of legal proceedings, and the prevention of such heinous crimes in the future.

The legal aftermath of Jeffrey Epstein's arrest and death has had wide-ranging consequences. It has provided an opportunity for victims to seek justice, but also raised serious concerns about the transparency and integrity of the justice system. The circumstances surrounding Epstein's death and the termination of the criminal case have fueled public distrust and scepticism.

Ongoing investigations and the pursuit of justice for Epstein's victims continue, but the case has exposed institutional failures and highlighted the need for systemic reforms to prevent similar cases and ensure the accountability of those involved in sex trafficking and exploitation.

What followed?

IN THE DARK REALM OF elite sex trafficking and exploitation, the revelations surrounding Jeffrey Epstein and his notorious network have left an indelible mark on society. The heinous crimes perpetrated by Epstein and his associates have brought to light a disturbing reality of abuse, manipulation, and the complicity of powerful individuals. As we reflect on this chapter, there are crucial lessons to be learned from this crime that must guide us towards a more just and accountable future.

One of the most significant lessons we can draw from the Epstein case is the urgent need for robust protection and support for victims of sex trafficking and exploitation. The stories of survivors who courageously shared their experiences have exposed the vulnerabilities they faced and the immense challenges they encountered in seeking justice. It is essential that our society provides comprehensive support systems, including safe spaces, counselling, legal aid, and resources for victims to rebuild their lives.

Furthermore, the Epstein case has starkly demonstrated the dangers of unchecked power and privilege. The involvement of influential individuals from various sectors highlights the insidious nature of exploitation and the willingness of some to turn a blind eye for personal gain or to maintain their own positions of power. It is incumbent upon us to challenge the culture of impunity that allows such abuse to persist and to hold those responsible accountable, regardless of their status or connections.

The Epstein case has also underscored the critical role of law enforcement and the justice system in investigating and prosecuting cases of elite sex trafficking and exploitation. The failures and controversies surrounding the handling of the Epstein case serve as reminders of the need for transparency, impartiality, and diligence in such high-profile investigations. There must be an unwavering commitment to pursuing the truth, even when the accused wield significant influence or resources.

Moreover, the Epstein case has revealed the flaws and vulnerabilities within regulatory systems that allowed his criminal activities to persist for an extended period. The case highlights the need for stronger oversight and scrutiny of financial transactions, particularly concerning suspicious transactions linked to sex trafficking networks. It is imperative to close the loopholes that enable the movement of illicit funds and to enhance cooperation among international law enforcement agencies to combat this transnational crime effectively.

The media's role in exposing and shedding light on elite sex trafficking and exploitation cannot be understated. Investigative journalism played a pivotal role in unearthing the depths of Epstein's network and bringing attention to the plight of his victims. It is crucial that journalists continue to pursue truth and hold powerful individuals accountable, even in the face of intimidation or resistance.

Lastly, the Epstein case serves as a call to action for society as a whole. We must challenge the normalisation of abuse and exploitation, and actively work towards creating a culture that supports survivors, educates the public about the signs of trafficking, and fosters empathy and compassion. It is our collective responsibility to create safer spaces and a world where individuals are valued and protected, regardless of their social status or vulnerability.

As we conclude this chapter on elite sex trafficking and exploitation, let us remember the survivors who have shown incredible strength and resilience in the face of unimaginable horrors. Their voices must be amplified, and their experiences must shape our actions. By learning from the Epstein case, we can strive for a society that is vigilant, compassionate, and committed to dismantling systems of abuse and ensuring justice for all. Together, let us stand against elite sex trafficking and exploitation, working towards a future where such crimes are eradicated, and every individual is treated with dignity and respect.

Conclusion

As we reach the end of our journey through the intricate world of financial crimes and scandals, it becomes clear that these issues extend far beyond the cases we have explored. They are symptomatic of larger systemic problems within our financial systems, requiring comprehensive reforms and a collective commitment to transparency and accountability. Unveiling the Shadows has aimed to shed light on the hidden truths, raise awareness, and ignite conversations that pave the way for change.

Reflecting on the stories of Bernard Madoff's audacious Ponzi scheme, Martha Stewart's insider trading conviction, the Panama Papers' exposé of money laundering networks, Lionel Messi's brush with tax evasion, and the horrors of elite sex trafficking associated with Jeffrey Epstein, we are confronted with the devastating consequences of these crimes. Lives destroyed, trust shattered, and the erosion of public faith in the integrity of our financial institutions.

Moving forward, it is essential to contemplate the broader implications and consider the following prompts:

1. What regulatory and legal reforms can be implemented to prevent and detect financial fraud and crimes more effectively?

2. How can we foster a culture of ethics and integrity within the financial industry?

3. What role does public awareness and education play in combating financial crimes?

4. How can governments and international organisations collaborate to tackle cross-border issues such as money laundering and tax evasion?

5. In what ways can the survivors and victims of financial crimes be supported, and their voices amplified?

By engaging in these discussions, we empower ourselves as a society to demand change, accountability, and justice. The journey into the shadows of financial crimes is not an easy one, but it is a necessary one if we are to safeguard our financial systems and protect the vulnerable from exploitation.

As we close the chapter on this book, let it serve as a reminder that the fight against financial crimes and scandals is an ongoing battle. It requires continuous vigilance, robust regulations, and a commitment from individuals, institutions, and governments to ensure that justice prevails. By working together, we can forge a future where the shadows are illuminated, and the light of transparency and integrity shines brightly.

Ultimately, the choice lies with us to dismantle the shadows, to demand a financial landscape built on trust, and to strive for a world where financial crimes and scandals are mere chapters in history, never to be repeated.

Don't miss out!

Visit the website below and you can sign up to receive emails whenever Edward Turner publishes a new book. There's no charge and no obligation.

https://books2read.com/r/B-A-SYIZ-YTKLC

BOOKS 2 READ

Connecting independent readers to independent writers.

Also by Edward Turner

Ghosts of Paris: Ten Haunted Places in the City of Love
Appalachian Nightmares: The Top 10 Creepy Creatures of the Mountains
Asia's Top Ten Cryptids: Legends, Sightings, and Theories
Beyond the Shadows: Unlocking the Mystery of Bigfoot
Evil Women in History: Uncovering the Gruesome Crimes of Ten Notorious Female Killers
Ghosts of London: Ten Haunted Places in The City
Ghosts of New York: Ten Haunted Places in The Big Apple
Ghosts of Oregon: The Top 10 Haunted Places You Must Visit
Ghosts of the Stage: Ten Hauntings at the Theatre
Missouri Nightmares: The Top 10 Chilling Legends
Mothman Unleashed: Into the Darkened Skies
North America's Top Ten Cryptids: Legends, Sightings, and Theories
Philly's Phantom Encounters: Exploring the City's Most Haunted Places
Secrets of the Deep: The Mystery of the Loch Ness Monster
Unsolved Mysteries: Delving into the Shadows of Infamous Murders and Enigmatic Killers
Unveiling the Shadows: A Journey into Financial Crimes and Scandals

About the Author

Edward Turner is a renowned author who specializes in exploring the realms of ghosts, the paranormal, and cryptids. With a captivating writing style and an insatiable curiosity for the unknown, Turner has garnered a dedicated following of readers who are captivated by his thrilling and eerie tales.

Born with an innate fascination for the supernatural, Turner has spent decades delving into the depths of paranormal phenomena, unearthing captivating stories and untangling mysteries that lie beyond the veil of the ordinary. His extensive research and meticulous attention to detail have earned him a reputation as a leading authority in the field.

Through his books, Turner expertly weaves together chilling accounts of encounters with ghosts, offering readers a glimpse into the ethereal world that coexists alongside our own. His ability to paint vivid portraits of spectral apparitions and convey the haunting atmosphere of haunted locations has made his works both spine-tingling and thought-provoking.

Turner's exploration of the paranormal doesn't stop at ghosts. He also dives into the fascinating world of cryptids—creatures that defy conventional explanation. His in-depth investigations into legendary creatures such as Bigfoot, the Loch Ness Monster, and the Chupacabra showcase his commitment to shedding light on these enigmatic beings.

With each page, Edward Turner's readers are drawn deeper into the enigmatic and unknown. His unique storytelling ability combined with his meticulous research has made him a sought-after author for those with an insatiable thirst for the supernatural. Whether delving into ghostly encounters or unraveling the mysteries of elusive cryptids, Turner's books offer a spine-chilling and immersive reading experience that leaves readers questioning the boundaries of our reality.

Edward Turner's works have earned critical acclaim and numerous accolades within the paranormal genre. He continues to explore the unexplained, captivating readers with his distinctive narrative style and unwavering dedication to unveiling the mysteries that lie hidden in the shadows.